MAKING
SHADOW
PUPPETS

Written by Jill Bryant and Catherine Heard

Illustrated by Laura Watson

KIDS CAN PRESS

In memory of Pat Chataway — J.B.

For Leah and Cate — C.H.

Text © 2002 Jill Bryant and Catherine Heard
Illustrations © 2002 Laura Watson

KIDS CAN DO IT and the 📖 logo are trademarks of Kids Can Press Ltd.

Many of the designations used by manufacturers and sellers to distinguish their products are claimed
as trademarks. Where those designations appear in this book and Kids Can Press Ltd. was aware of
a trademark claim, the designations have been printed in initial capital letters (e.g., Styrofoam).

Neither the Publisher nor the Author shall be liable for any damage that may be caused or sustained
as a result of conducting any of the activities in this book without specifically following instructions,
conducting the activities without proper supervision, or ignoring the cautions contained in the book.

Kids Can Press acknowledges the support of the Government of Canada,
through the BPIDP, for our publishing activity.

Published in Canada by   Published in the U.S. by
Kids Can Press Ltd.   Kids Can Press Ltd.
29 Birch Avenue   2250 Military Road
Toronto, ON M4V 1E2   Tonawanda, NY 14150

www.kidscanpress.com

Edited by Maggie MacDonald
Designed by Karen Powers
Photography by Frank Baldassarra

Puppets on page 8 courtesy of David Powell of Puppetmongers, Toronto,
and puppet on page 9 courtesy of Harry Wisebaum.

Printed and bound in Singapore
The hardcover edition of this book is smyth sewn casebound.
The paperback edition of this book is limp sewn with a drawn-on cover.

CM 02 0 9 8 7 6 5 4 3 2
CM PA 02 0 9 8 7 6 5 4 3 2 1

National Library of Canada Cataloguing in Publication Data

Bryant, Jill
Making shadow puppets

(Kids can do it)

ISBN 1-55337-028-7 (bound)   ISBN 1-55337-029-5 (pbk.)

1. Shadow puppets — Juvenile literature. 2. Shadow plays — Juvenile literature.
I. Heard, Catherine. II. Watson, Laura, 1968–. III. Title. IV. Series.

PN1979.S5B79 2002   j791.5'3   C2001-903442-3

Kids Can Press is a Corus™ Entertainment company

Contents

Introduction

You may know how to make hand shadows on your bedroom wall or the side of a tent, but what is a traditional shadow puppet? Shadow puppets are flat figures held up and controlled by thin rods or sticks attached to their bodies and limbs. Some puppets have many tiny cutout shapes that let bits of light through and create breathtaking silhouettes.

This book includes instructions for making nine wonderful shadow puppets and two types of shadow screens. The traceable template shapes on page 40 will help you draw the parts of the puppets. Watch how the flat shapes of shadow puppets come alive when you move them behind a screen! Rods attached to parts of the puppets let you make them dance, wave and leap. Act out a familiar story with the puppets, or create a play of your own. Have fun performing shadow puppet plays for your family and friends.

With the shadow puppets in this book, you can make animals and people that are easy to recognize by their silhouettes. Many designs include suggestions for making other puppets. Once you have made the horse, for example, you can use the same method to make other four-legged creatures, such as a giraffe, a dog or a cat.

The templates on page 40 will help you make puppet bodies with correct proportions. It's amazing how many creatures start with these simple oval shapes. Later on, you can make puppets by drawing their outlines without using the templates.

Jazz up your puppets with different decorative techniques. Who says shadows have to be black? You can make colors show through the screen with a special technique using layers of colored tissue paper and glue, or pieces of colored cellophane.

Materials

You can find many of the basic materials to make shadow puppets around your house. Other materials are easy to find at craft or office supply stores.

Bristol Board

Any color of bristol board is fine for making shadow puppets, but if you are decorating your puppets, choose a light color for best results.

Hole Punch

Push the paper as far into the punch as possible so that the hole isn't too close to the edge. Squeeze the handles together and — presto — a hole appears!

Paper Fasteners

Use these small, metal devices to connect the different parts of the puppets. For example, paper fasteners join a leg to a hip and an arm to a shoulder. They are also used to form knees and elbows. These connections between two parts are called joints. You can find paper fasteners at an office supply store.

How to Attach Paper Fasteners

Once you have punched a hole in both pieces of bristol board that you want to connect to make a joint, line up the holes one on top of the other and push a closed paper fastener through the hole. Separate the two pieces of metal and push them apart until they lie flat. Make sure the joint moves easily and isn't too tight.

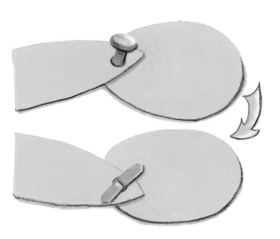

Wooden Rods

The wooden rods are the parts that you hold on to when you make the shadow puppets perform. You can use small bamboo skewers, 0.5 cm (¼ in.) dowels or thick plastic drinking straws. If you use skewers with a pointy end, ask an adult to cut this end off with gardening shears.

Tape

Masking tape or sticky tape works best for attaching the rods to the backs of the shadow puppets.

How to Attach Rods

Tear off a small piece (2.5 cm or 1 in.) of tape. Try not to touch the sticky side of the tape too much. Place half of the piece of tape on the puppet in the spot where you want the rod to attach. Then stick the other half to the wooden rod. Repeat this on the other side of the wooden rod. Wrap an extra piece of tape around the tape on the rod to make the connection stronger. Rub all the pieces of tape firmly to make sure they are secure. Now you have made a special hinge on the back of the puppet.

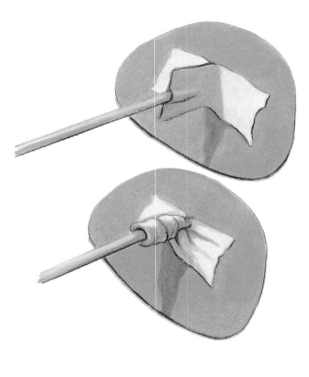

Additional Materials

- crayons, markers, pencil crayons, poster paints and paintbrushes, ink or food coloring

- glitter, paper from magazines, tissue paper, silver paper or aluminum foil

- string, ribbon or yarn

- pipe cleaners

- a Styrofoam tray

- cellophane, acetate. You might find cellophane around the house. It is a lightweight plastic that is often used for wrapping gift baskets. You can purchase acetate (heavier plastic) at craft or office supply stores. Both cellophane and acetate are available in colored or clear versions.

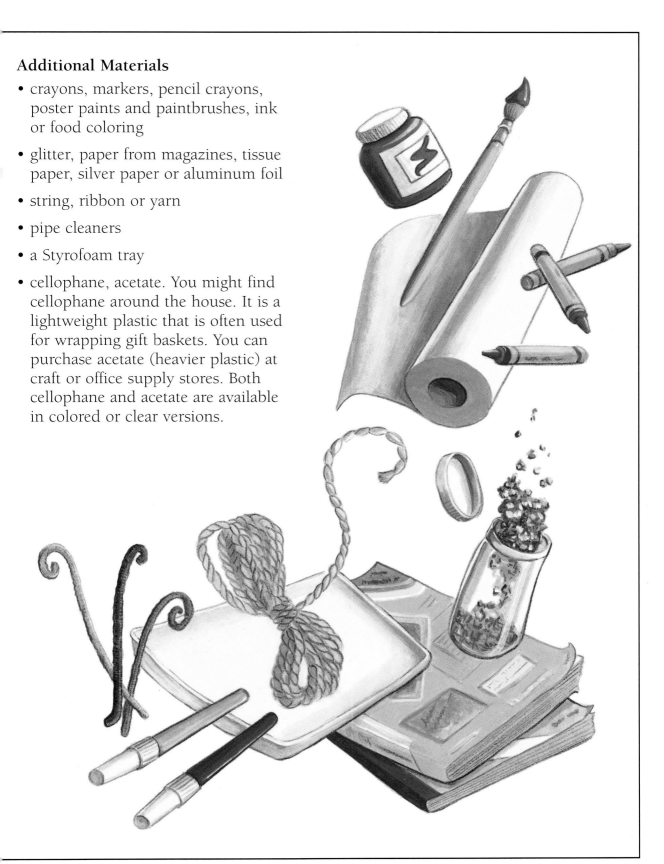

Historical Background

Shadow puppets are found in many different cultures, but they are best known in China, Indonesia and Turkey. In both Indonesian and Turkish shadow puppet plays, there is one master puppeteer. This puppeteer controls all the puppets while an apprentice helps out behind the screen. Shows in China and India take advantage of more hands by using several puppeteers.

You can become a professional shadow puppeteer by apprenticing under an experienced master or studying at a special school.

Music is an important part of shadow puppet performances. In Indonesia, there is a singer and up to 20 musicians. Special days, such as weddings or birth celebrations, are often honored with a shadow puppet performance.

Seating Arrangements

Shadow puppets are beautiful works of art. Traditionally, in small Indonesian homes, the family and their guests sat behind the screen, where they could see the puppets in full color and watch the puppeteer at work. Other villagers sat on the shadow side. More often, in larger homes or palaces, men sat on the puppeteer's side and women sat on the shadow side.

Upper-class lady — Indonesia

Tiger — China

Warrior on Horseback — China

Characters

As a rule, traditional shadow puppet plays from Asia feature well-known characters (stock figures) from each culture's stories and legends. In each play, the same characters find themselves in a different situation, much like in today's sitcoms on television. For example, the hero of Turkish shadow puppet plays is Karagoz, or Black-Eye. He is a funny, uneducated man who often gets himself out of sticky situations by tricking his rivals.

Karagoz — Turkey

Map of the World

This map shows the parts of the world where shadow puppets originated.

Traditional Materials

The bodies of traditional shadow puppets are made from the hides of animals such as water buffalo, pigs, goats, donkeys or fish. The rods are made of buffalo horn, bamboo or wood. In the past, the hides were rubbed, dried in the sun, soaked, stretched and dried again. Then the leather was scraped and polished.

After designs were engraved onto the leather, the craftsperson cut out these intricate shapes and decorated the puppets with different colors of paint.

Tools

Craftspeople have always used interesting tools to make traditional shadow puppets. Metal carving tools, including small chisels with different-shaped tips and hole punches, are used to cut intricate patterns into the puppets.

1 Greece
2 Turkey
3 Egypt
4 Iran
5 India
6 Thailand
7 Cambodia
8 Malaysia
9 Indonesia
10 China

Snake

*Wriggle this snake smoothly across
the shadow puppet screen.*

YOU WILL NEED

- a piece of bristol board,
20 cm x 30 cm (8 in. x 12 in.)
- 4 paper fasteners
- 2 thin rods, 30 cm (12 in.)
- paper from magazines (optional)
- glue (optional)
- a pencil, an eraser, scissors, tape,
a hole punch
- templates (see page 40)

1 Using template 2, draw a small
oval on the bristol board. Draw
the shape of a mouth on the oval. Cut
out this shape.

2 To make a tongue, draw the shape
of a letter Y on the bristol board,
cut it out and tape it to the back of the
puppet's mouth.

3 Using template 3, draw four long
ovals on the bristol board. Cut
them out.

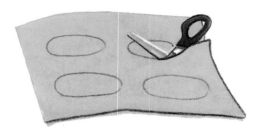

4 Make the tail by cutting the end of one of the ovals from step 3 into a point.

5 Lay the pieces out in the shape of the puppet. Mark X's where the paper fasteners will go. Use the hole punch (page 5) to make a hole at each X. Put your puppet together with paper fasteners (page 5).

6 On the back of the puppet, attach one rod (page 6) to the middle of the snake's head and one to its tail.

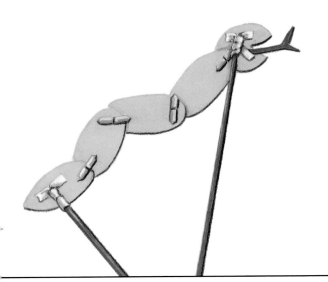

7 If you like, decorate your snake by cutting scale shapes from glossy magazine paper and gluing them onto the bristol board. (You can decorate your puppet using other materials, if you prefer.)

OTHER IDEAS

Adapt this snake pattern to make caterpillar and worm puppets.

Flying bird

With a little practice, you can make this flying bird shadow puppet swoop and dip in the sky.

YOU WILL NEED

- a piece of bristol board,
20 cm x 30 cm (8 in. x 12 in.)
- 2 paper fasteners
- 3 thin rods, 30 cm (12 in.)
- crayons (optional)
- ink or food coloring (optional)
- a pencil, an eraser, scissors,
a hole punch, tape
- templates (see page 40)

1 Using template 2, draw a small oval on the bristol board. Draw the bird's head at the top of the oval and its feet at the bottom of the oval. Cut out this shape.

2 Using template 1, draw a large oval on the bristol board. Cut the oval in half. Cut the straight edges of the oval in the shapes of feathers.

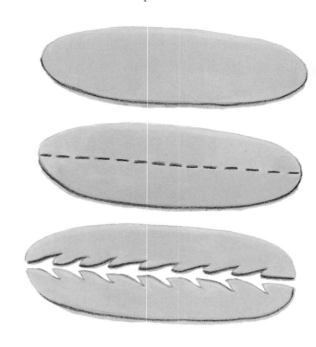

3 Lay the pieces out in the shape of the puppet. Mark **X**'s where the paper fasteners will go. Use the hole punch (page 5) to make a hole at each **X**. Put your puppet together with paper fasteners (page 5).

4 On the back of the puppet, attach one rod (page 6) to the middle of the bird's head and one to each of its wings.

5 If you like, decorate your bird by coloring it with crayons and then painting over the crayon with ink or food coloring mixed with water. (You can decorate your puppet using other materials, if you prefer.)

OTHER IDEAS

This basic pattern is all you need to make a butterfly or another insect.

Horse

Practice making this majestic horse gallop into the sunset.

YOU WILL NEED

- a piece of bristol board, 40 cm x 40 cm (16 in. x 16 in.)
- 9 paper fasteners
- 2 thin rods, 30 cm (12 in.)
- poster paints and paintbrushes (optional)
- a piece of ribbon or yarn, 38 cm (15 in.)
- a piece of yarn, 75 cm (30 in.) (optional)
- glue (optional)
- a pencil, an eraser, scissors, tape, a hole punch
- templates (see page 40)

1 Using template 1, draw a large oval on the bristol board. Draw a tail at one end of the oval. Cut out the shape.

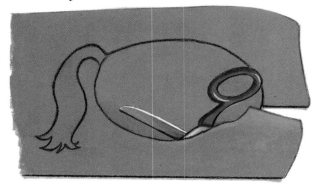

2 Using template 2, draw a small oval on the bristol board. Add a long neck, ears and a muzzle to create your horse's head. Cut out the shape.

3 Using template 3, draw eight long ovals on the bristol board. Draw hooves at the bottom of four of the ovals. Cut out the shapes.

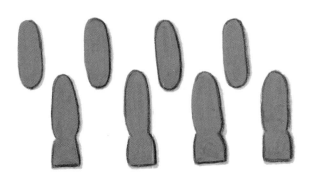

4 Lay the pieces out in the shape of the puppet. Mark **X**'s where the paper fasteners will go. Use the hole punch (page 5) to make a hole at each **X**. Put your puppet together with paper fasteners (page 5).

5 On the back of the puppet, attach one rod (page 6) to the middle of the horse's head and one to the middle of its body.

6 If you like, paint your horse with poster paints. (You can decorate your puppet using other materials, if you prefer.) Let dry.

7 Make a bridle with the ribbon as shown. Glue or tape the bridle to the horse. Make the reins long enough so that the horse's head can move freely.

8 If you like, you can make the horse's mane, tail and forelock out of yarn. Cut 20 to 30 short lengths (about 2.5 cm, or 1 in.) of yarn. Use white glue to attach them to the back of the horse's neck, tail and forehead.

OTHER IDEAS

You can make any four-legged animal with this basic pattern. For a giraffe, make the neck and legs longer. For a dog or cat, make the neck and legs shorter.

Jester

*This medieval clown loves to joke
around and perform for royalty.*

YOU WILL NEED

- a piece of bristol board,
40 cm x 40 cm (16 in. x 16 in.)
- 8 paper fasteners
- 3 thin rods, 30 cm (12 in.)
- pencil crayons (optional)
- glitter (optional)
- glue (optional)
- a pencil, an eraser, scissors, a hole punch, tape
- templates (see page 40)

1 Using template 1, draw a large oval on the bristol board. Then, using template 2, draw a small oval just above it, leaving about 1 cm (1/2 in.) between the two ovals.

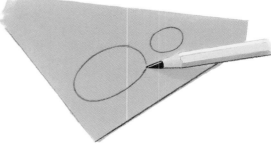

2 On the small oval, draw the shape of the jester's face and hat. On the large oval, draw the shape of his tunic. Draw a neck connecting his head to his body. Make it at least 3 cm (1 1/4 in.) wide to help prevent it from tearing. Cut out this shape.

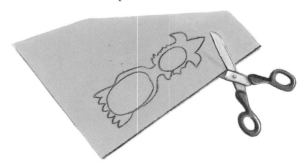

3 Using template 3, draw four long ovals on the bristol board. These will be the arms. Add hands and the shape of the jester's sleeves to two of these ovals. Cut them out.

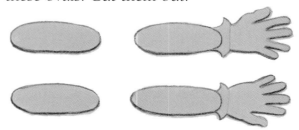

4 Using template 3, draw four more long ovals on the bristol board. These will be the legs. Add boots to two of these ovals and the shape of the jester's pants to the other two. Cut them out.

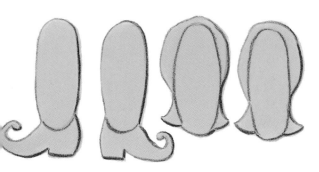

5 Lay the pieces out in the shape of the puppet. Mark X's where the paper fasteners will go. Use the hole punch (page 5) to make a hole at each X. Put your puppet together with paper fasteners (page 5).

6 On the back of the puppet, attach one rod (page 6) to the middle of the jester's body and one to each of his arms.

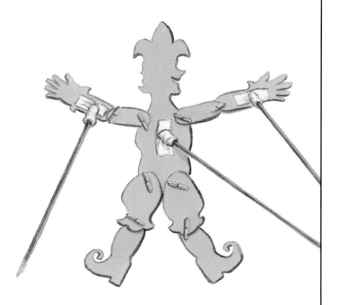

7 If you like, color your jester with pencil crayons. Put glue on the hat, tunic and other places that you want to sparkle. Sprinkle on the glitter before the glue dries. (You can decorate your puppet using other materials, if you prefer.)

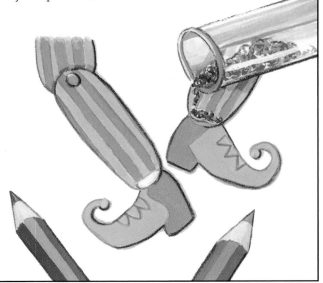

Monster

Give your friends a scare with this furry monster shadow puppet with glowing eyes.

YOU WILL NEED

- a piece of bristol board,
  40 cm x 40 cm (16 in. x 16 in.)
- small pieces of colored cellophane
- 3 paper fasteners
- 2 thin rods, 30 cm (12 in.)
- a metallic gold or silver marker (optional)
- a pencil, an eraser, scissors,
  a hole punch, tape
- templates (see page 40)

1 Using template 2, draw two small ovals touching each other on the bristol board. Draw the shape of the monster's face and fur around the two ovals. Cut out this shape.

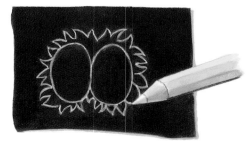

2 Draw the eyes and mouth on the face. Cut out these shapes. (Use the pointy end of a pencil to start the hole for your scissors.) Tape colored cellophane over the eye and mouth holes.

3 Using template 1, draw a large oval on the bristol board. Draw the shape of the monster's body and tail around the large oval. Cut this out.

4 Using template 3, draw two long ovals on the bristol board. Draw the monster's feet at the bottom of these ovals. Cut out these shapes.

5 Lay the pieces out in the shape of the puppet. Mark **X**'s where the paper fasteners will go. Use the hole punch (page 5) to make a hole at each **X**. Put your puppet together with paper fasteners (page 5).

6 On the back of the puppet, attach one rod (page 6) to the middle of the monster's head and one to the middle of its body. Be careful not to cover the monster's eyes or mouth when you attach the rod to the head.

7 If you like, decorate your monster with a metallic marker. (You can decorate your puppet using other materials, if you prefer.)

OTHER IDEAS

Transform the monster pattern into a bird with a few simple changes. Presto!

- Using the large oval for the body, and the small oval for the head, you can make a bird.

- By adding three long narrow ovals for a neck and long legs, you will have an ostrich.

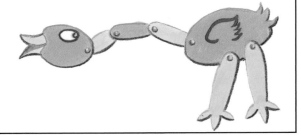

Donkey prince

This shadow puppet with a changeable head is modeled after a traditional puppet from Turkey.

YOU WILL NEED

- a piece of bristol board,
40 cm x 40 cm (16 in. x 16 in.)
- 9 paper fasteners
- a piece of string or yarn, 4 cm (1½ in.)
- 4 thin rods, 30 cm (12 in.)
- markers (optional)
- a pencil, an eraser, scissors,
a hole punch, tape
- templates (see page 40)

1 Using template 2, draw a small oval on the bristol board. Turn the same template sideways and draw another small oval above the first one, leaving 2 cm (¾ in.) of space between them.

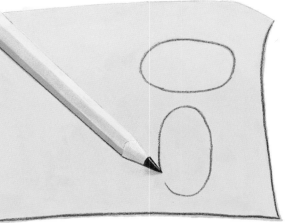

2 On the upright oval, draw the shape of the prince's face, hair and crown. On the sideways oval, draw the shape of the donkey's face and ears. Draw a neck connecting the two heads. Make it at least 3 cm (1¼ in.) wide, to help prevent it from tearing. Cut out this shape.

3 Using template 1, draw a large oval on the bristol board. Draw the shape of the prince's jacket on this oval. Cut out this shape.

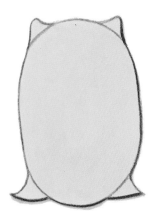

4 Using template 3, draw four long ovals on the bristol board. These will be the arms. Add hands and the shape of the prince's sleeves to two of these ovals. Cut these out.

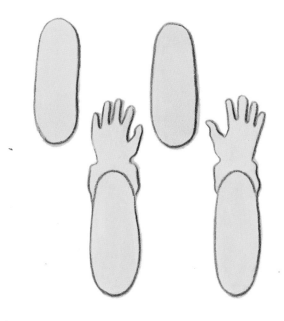

5 Using template 3, draw four more long ovals on the bristol board. These will be the legs. Add boots and the shape of the prince's pants to two of these ovals. Cut these out.

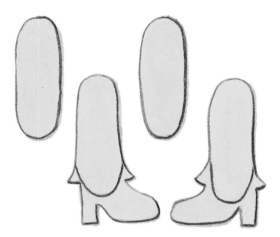

6 Lay the pieces out in the shape of the puppet. Mark **X**'s where the paper fasteners will go. Use the hole punch (page 5) to make a hole at each **X**. Put your puppet together with paper fasteners (page 5).

Instructions continue on the next page ☞

7 Tape one end of the string to the back of the donkey's head. Tape the other end of the string to a rod. There should be only about 0.5 cm (¼ in.) of string between head and the rod.

9 If you like, color your prince and donkey with markers. (You can decorate your puppet using other materials, if you prefer.)

8 Attach one rod (page 6) to the body (below the hidden prince's head) and one rod to each of the arms using the standard method.

10 Use the rod on the back of the donkey's head to switch from one head to another. You can turn the donkey into a prince, and the prince into a donkey. From in front of the shadow screen, it looks like magic!

Robot

The eye of this robot blinks on and off, and the gear turns at the top of his head when he thinks!

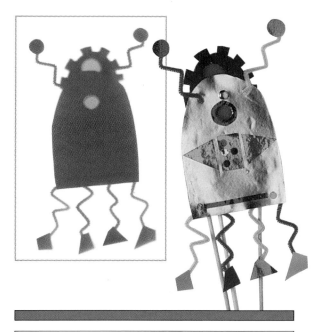

YOU WILL NEED

- a piece of bristol board, 40 cm x 40 cm (16 in. x 16 in.)
- a penny
- a paper fastener
- 3 thin rods, 30 cm (12 in.)
- a piece of string or yarn, 4 cm (1½ in.)
- 3 pipe cleaners cut in half
- silver paper or aluminum foil (optional)
- a pencil, an eraser, scissors, a hole punch, tape
- templates (see page 40)

1 Using template 2, draw a small oval on the bristol board. Cut the edge so that it looks like a gear.

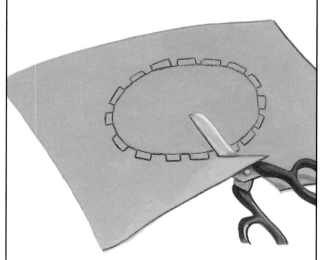

2 Use the pointy end of a pencil to carefully make a small hole in the middle of the oval. Trace the penny 0.5 cm (¼ in.) above and 0.5 cm. (¼ in.) below this hole. Cut out these shapes.

Instructions continue on the next page ☞

3 Using template 1, draw a large oval on the bristol board. Trim the bottom to make a flat edge.

5 Attach the small oval to the large oval using the paper fastener (page 5).

4 Make a hole at the top of the oval using the hole punch (page 5). Trace the penny 0.5 cm (1/4 in.) underneath this hole. Using the pointy end of a pencil to start the hole for your scissors, cut it out.

6 Attach two rods (page 6) to the back of the puppet. They should be about 2.5 cm (1 in.) apart. (Use two rods to hold your puppet stable when you turn the top oval to make the gear turn and the light blink.)

7 Tape one end of the string to the back of the small oval. Tape the other end of the string to the third rod. There should be only about 0.5 cm (¼ in.) of string between the small oval and the rod.

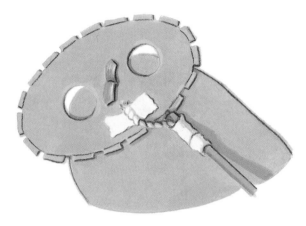

8 Bend the pipe cleaners into funny shapes. Use scraps of bristol board to make robot parts. Glue the parts to the ends of the pipe cleaners, then glue the pipe cleaners to the front of the robot. If you like, decorate your puppet using silver paper. (You can decorate your puppet using other materials, if you prefer.)

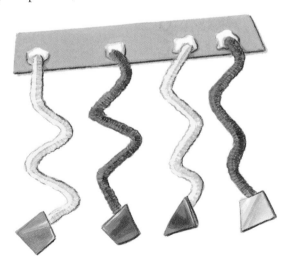

OTHER IDEAS

If you want to be really fancy, tape colored cellophane over the holes in the small oval. Covering each hole with a different color will make the robot's light look like it is blinking different colors when you turn the wheel!

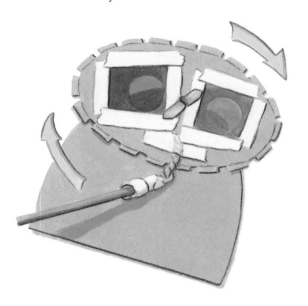

You can make other machines with parts that turn. Just use string to attach the rod to the part of the puppet that turns.

Princess

Make a beautiful dress for the princess by punching out holes in an interesting pattern. This traditional Indonesian technique creates a wonderful effect.

1 Using template 2, draw two small ovals on the bristol board, one above the other, leaving about 1 cm (½ in.) between them. Draw the shape of the princess's face, hair, crown and blouse on the ovals. Draw her neck between the ovals. Make it at least 3 cm (1 ¼ in.) wide to prevent it from tearing. Cut out this shape.

2 Using template 1, draw a large oval on the bristol board. Square off the bottom to make it look like a skirt. You can make a fancy edge, if you like. Cut out this shape.

3 Using template 3, draw four long ovals on the bristol board. These will be the arms. Add hands to two of these ovals and the shape of the princess's sleeves to the other two. Cut them out.

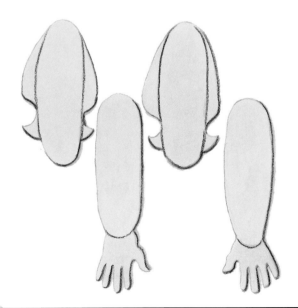

4 Using template 3, draw two more long ovals on the bristol board. These will be the legs. Add pretty shoes to the bottom of these ovals. Cut them out.

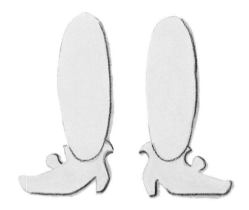

5 Lay the pieces out in the shape of the puppet. Mark **X**'s where the paper fasteners will go. Use the hole punch (page 5) to make a hole at each **X**. Put your puppet together with paper fasteners (page 5).

Instructions continue on the next page ☞

6 On the back of the puppet, attach one rod (page 6) to the middle of the princess's body and one rod to each of her arms.

7 If you like, put a Styrofoam tray under your puppet and use the pointy end of your pencil to poke small holes through in a lacy pattern. Color your puppet with markers, if you wish. (You can decorate your puppet using other materials, if you prefer.)

Fairy

Colored shadows were created in China by painting the puppets with dyes, then rubbing them with oil on both sides. This technique allowed the light to pass through.

YOU WILL NEED

- a cardboard box
- a plastic bag
- white glue (or Mod Podge)
- water
- a container for mixing glue and water
- a paintbrush
- white tissue paper
- light-colored tissue paper
- 2 paper fasteners
- 2 thin rods, 30 cm (12 in.)
- a pencil, an eraser, scissors, a hole punch, tape
- templates (see page 40)

Note: *You must wait overnight after step 2 to allow the tissue paper to dry completely. It will be worth the wait because this puppet casts a magical colored shadow onto the shadow puppet screen.*

1 Cut one of the sides out of the cardboard box and trim it to approximately 30 cm x 40 cm (12 in. x 16 in.). Cut a slightly smaller piece of plastic from the plastic bag. Stretch it smoothly over the cardboard and tape it securely.

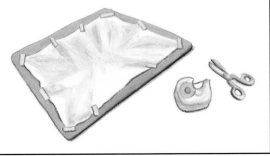

Instructions continue on the next page ☞ 29

2 Mix equal amounts of glue and water (or use undiluted Mod Podge). Cover the plastic bag with a layer of white tissue paper. Paint this layer with the glue and water mixture. Tear the colored tissue paper into 5 cm x 5 cm (2 in. x 2 in.) pieces. Layer these pieces onto the white tissue paper and paint with more glue and water. Let dry overnight.

3 Using template 2, draw two small ovals, one above the other, on the paper you have made. They should overlap slightly.

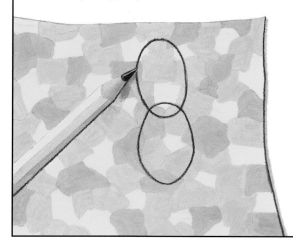

4 Draw the shape of the fairy's face and hair on the top oval. On the bottom oval, draw the shape of the fairy's wings, clothes and legs. Cut out this shape.

Helpful hint: *The wings are the shape of the small oval cut in half.*

5 Using template 3, draw two long ovals. These will be the arms. Trim them to a narrower shape (1.5 cm or 5/8 in. wide), then add hands. Don't forget to give your fairy a magic wand! Cut out the arms.

6 Lay the pieces out in the shape of the puppet. Use a pencil to mark **X**'s where the paper fasteners will go. Use the hole punch (page 5) to make a hole at each **X**. Put your puppet together with paper fasteners (page 5).

7 On the back of the puppet, attach one rod (page 6) to the fairy's head and one to each of its arms.

OTHER IDEAS

You can use this technique to make a ghost puppet. Boo!

1. Follow steps 1 to 3 of the fairy puppet.

2. Draw the shape of the ghost's body over the two ovals.

3. Follow steps 5 to 7 of the fairy puppet, but omit the wand.

Making a box screen

You can make a simple box-screen theater that can be used in any room. All you need is a small table to place it on.

- a large cardboard box
- a small table
- lightweight white paper (bond or tracing paper) or lightweight white fabric (cotton sheeting or muslin) big enough to cover the screen side of the box
- colored paper, markers or other materials for decorating
- a tablecloth or sheet
- scissors, tape or glue

1 Decide which side of the box you would like the screen to be on. Cut off the opposite side of the box so that the box is about 15 cm (6 in.) deep. Make sure the box will sit securely on a tabletop on one of the long sides. You may need to add a piece of cardboard to the back to prevent the box from toppling over.

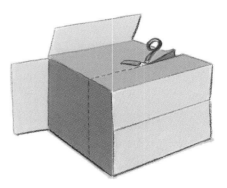

2 Cut a large window for the screen, leaving a border of about 5 cm (2 in.) to frame the screen area.

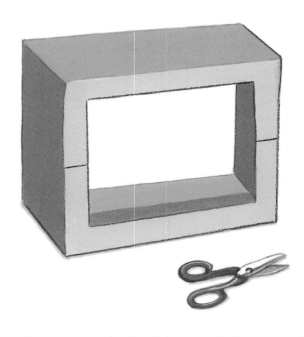

3 Cut the paper or fabric so that it is about 2.5 cm (1 in.) larger than the size of the opening. Place the paper or fabric over the window and tape or glue it to the inside of the box. (Glue works best for fabric.) Make sure the paper or fabric doesn't have any wrinkles.

4 Decorate the outside of the box screen with colored paper, markers or other fun objects or craft supplies you find around the house.

5 Cover a small table with a tablecloth that hangs down to the floor, so that you can hide behind the table and not be seen by the audience. Set the box screen on the table.

LIGHTING TIPS

A small desk light with a base is a good source of light. Set the light on a chair or small table behind the screen, on the same side as the puppeteers. Point the lightbulb directly at the back of the screen in the center of the area where most of the action will take place.

For best results, turn out all other lights in the room. Take turns looking at the shadows from the audience's point of view. This will help you make clear silhouettes.

POSITIONING THE PUPPETS

Usually, shadow puppets perform up close to the back of the screen. This makes a sharp shadow image. Try pulling the puppets back slightly from the screen. What happens?

Making a doorway screen

Doorway-screen theaters are perfect for performing in your home. They work best if you plan to practice and perform your play in the same doorway. The dark bottom half of the screen hides the puppeteers from the audience's view.

YOU WILL NEED

- a tape measure
- a piece of white sheeting or muslin to fit in half of a doorway, approximately 90 cm x 105 cm (36 in. x 42 in.)
- a piece of black fabric to fit in half of a doorway, approximately 90 cm x 105 cm (36 in. x 42 in.)
- a spool of white thread, a spool of black thread, a sewing needle, pins, a pin cushion, sharp sewing scissors
- a sewing machine (optional)
- an iron and ironing board
- 3 pieces of Velcro with adhesive backing, each 2.5 (1 in.)

1 Measure the doorway that you plan to use for your shadow puppet screen. Ask an adult to help you measure the height. Add 10 cm (4 in.) to the width and 20 cm (8 in.) to the height so that there won't be any gaps at the edges of the screen. (This allows for the seams as well.)

2 Divide the height in half and ask an adult to help you cut two pieces of fabric to fit this size, one white and one black.

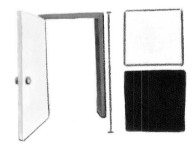

3 Put the tops of the pieces of the fabric together, with the white piece under the black piece, and sew with black thread. This will join the two pieces. Use a basic running stitch when sewing by hand. (You can also ask an adult to help you use a sewing machine.)

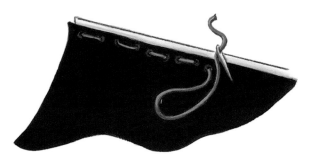

4 Sew around the outside of the screen using black thread to sew the black fabric and white thread to sew the white fabric. Create finished seams at the top, bottom and sides. To make a seam, fold each edge over once and iron. Repeat with each edge. Pin the seams and sew with a basic running stitch. Remove the pins.

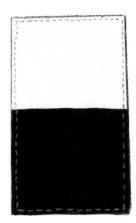

Note: *Always ask an adult to help you use an iron.*

5 Sew one piece of Velcro to each end of the top of the screen and one in the middle. Ask an adult to help you stick the adhesive backing side onto the door frame in the same positions.

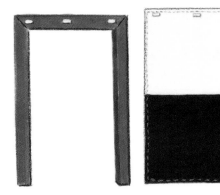

6 Hang the screen in the doorway, position your light behind the screen, turn out the lights and practice your shadow puppet play!

Putting on a play

BRAINSTORMING

Now that you have made lots of shadow puppets, you can think about putting on a play. Look at the characters you have created. Can you think of a story using these puppets?

Choose a setting for your play. Do you want a play set in modern times, long ago or in the future? Pick a hero, a heroine and a villain. Create a problem, such as a prince waking up with long, floppy ears and the head of a donkey after playing mean tricks on his sister. Find a way to have one character solve the problem. This will form the plot of the story or play.

WRITING A SCRIPT

If you like, write out the lines for each character and decide what the narrator will say. This is called a script. Or you can make up what the puppets will say as you rehearse. This method is called "ad-libbing." No matter which method you choose, the more times you practice, the better your play will be.

THE NARRATOR

The narrator can explain what is happening at the beginning of the play and between scenes. For example, the narrator might begin a play saying:

"Long ago, there lived an evil, scaly sea snake. The snake spent every day circling around the castle in the foamy green moat. One day, the prince and princess, who lived in the castle, spotted the snake and decided that this creature belonged in the castle's huge glass aquarium."

This introduces the play and tells the audience a little bit about what is going on before the puppeteers begin the performance.

ASSIGNING ROLES

How many puppeteers are there? It may be possible to double up the smaller roles so that some puppeteers have more than one role. For example, you could put on a puppet play with just two puppeteers and six puppets if each person controls three puppets. Even if you are normally a quiet person, you might enjoy performing the loud villain puppet. Experiment with different puppets and see which ones you like performing the best.

WHAT'S IT CALLED?

Here is a great way to introduce your play. You'll need a sheet of clear acetate (heavier plastic) and a water-soluble marker. Write the name of the play in big letters on the plastic and hold it up against the back of the screen with the words facing the audience before you begin the performance.

This effect will remind your audience of watching a movie. It looks great!

Props and scenery

Puppets can pass small props, such as an apple, a bag of gold or a magic carpet, to each other. Once you have an idea for a play, you will know what props to make.

MAKING PROPS

Using bristol board, cut out the shapes of the props. Make sure the props are big enough to be seen by the audience. Attach a thin rod to the back of each prop so you can move it from puppet to puppet.

MAKING SCENERY

Scenery is optional, but it will add atmosphere to your performance. Scenery tells the audience where the action is taking place. Some examples of scenery you can make are a lighthouse, a forest or a city street.

You can make your scenery simple or detailed. A single castle turret is all you need for a castle scene. But if you are feeling ambitious, you can create a more complex version.

SCENERY DETAILS

Windows and other cutout patterns will jazz up your scenery. Use the pointy end of a pencil to poke a hole where you'd like to make a window. Then, starting at that hole, use scissors to cut out the shape of the window. Tape colored cellophane (lightweight plastic) over the openings. This will create a mysterious glow from inside the lighthouse.

SPECIAL EFFECTS

Cast a colored shadow on the screen with props and scenery that light shines through. To make a crystal ball, a rainbow or a shooting star, use the technique described in steps 1 and 2 on pages 29 and 30.

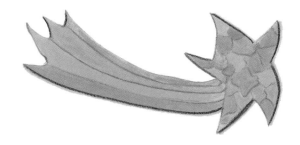

USING PLASTIC

Cut out simple scenery pieces, such as the sun, some clouds or the moon, from colored acetate (heavier plastic). Tape these to the back of the screen with sticky tape.

Using a sheet of clear acetate and water-soluble markers, you can draw rain, snow or even a rainbow! Hang the plastic sheet on the back of the screen with a few pieces of sticky tape. You can use the same sheet for a different play by erasing the picture with water and a soft cloth.

Create instant scenery by drawing the entire background on a sheet of clear acetate. Secure the sheet to the back of the screen with a few pieces of sticky tape. This keeps your hands free for moving the shadow puppets.

HAVE FUN!

Preparing for a performance can be lots of fun. Invite your friends and family to come to watch your shadow puppet play. Enjoy the show!

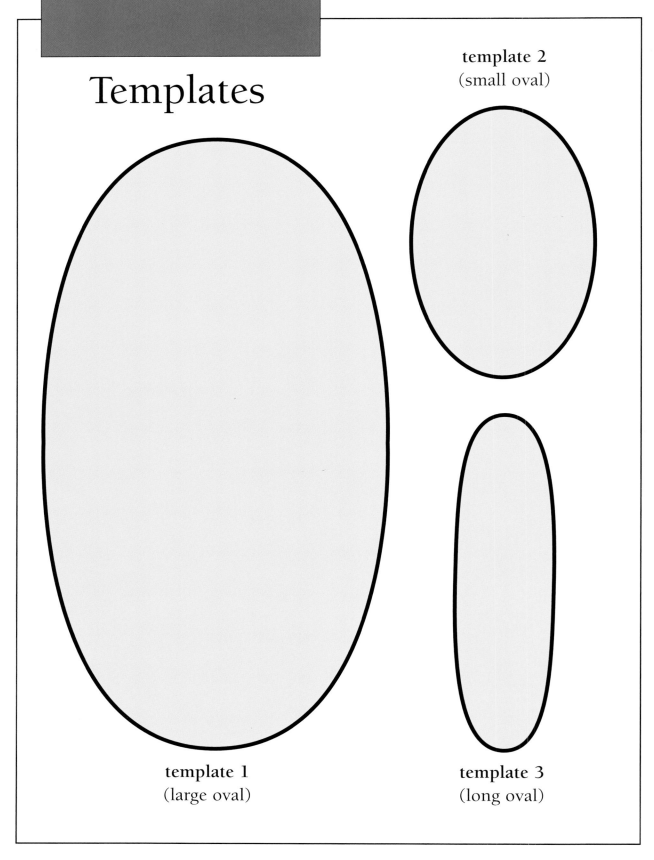

Templates

template 2
(small oval)

template 1
(large oval)

template 3
(long oval)